THE KENT &
EAST SUSSEX RAILWAY

HUGH NIGHTINGALE

HALSGROVE

First published in Great Britain in 2008

Title page: P-Class No.753 pilots Terrier 32678 storming up Tenterden Bank with returning 1.45pm Santa Special, seen just below Cranbrook Road crossing in the afternoon sunshine of Sunday 4th December 2005.

British Library Cataloguing-in-Publication Data
A CIP record for this title is available from the British Library

ISBN 978 1 84114 772 7

HALSGROVE
Halsgrove House,
Ryelands Industrial Estate,
Bagley Road, Wellington, Somerset TA21 9PZ
Tel: 01823 653777   Fax: 01823 216796
email: sales@halsgrove.com
website: www.halsgrove.com

Printed and bound by Grafiche Flaminia, Italy

DEDICATION

This book is dedicated to the staff and volunteers, past and present, of the Kent and East Sussex Railway.

"The consciousness of belonging, vitally, to something beyond individuality; of being part of a personality that reaches we know not where, in space and time, greatens the heart to the limit of the soul's ideal, and builds out the supreme of character."
Joshua Lawrence Chamberlain, 3rd October 1863

No.14 "Charwelton", a Manning Wardle 0-6-0ST of 1917, hauls a special charter of the "Wealden Pullman" up Tenterden Bank, east of Cranbrook Road, approaching the shallow cutting below the Home Signal, on 27th November 1982. A matter of minutes later a thick late autumn fog descended.

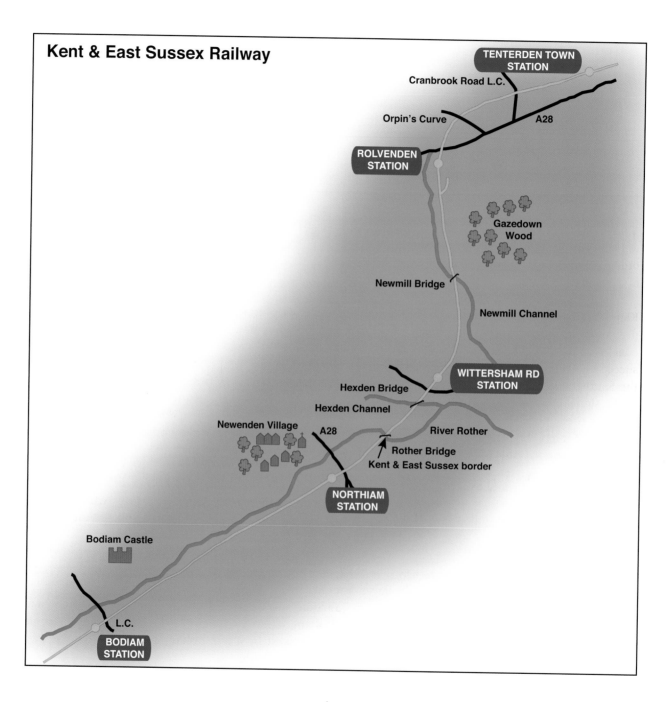

Kent & East Sussex Railway

TENTERDEN TOWN STATION

Cranbrook Road L.C.

Orpin's Curve

A28

ROLVENDEN STATION

Gazedown Wood

Newmill Bridge

Newmill Channel

WITTERSHAM RD STATION

Hexden Bridge

Hexden Channel

River Rother

Newenden Village

A28

Rother Bridge
Kent & East Sussex border

NORTHIAM STATION

Bodiam Castle

L.C.

BODIAM STATION

INTRODUCTION

In August 1862, a frustrated Colonel Adelbert Ames of the 20th Maine Volunteers was forced to describe his newly formed Federal infantry unit as a *hell* of a regiment. Dress was informal, to say the least, orders were interpreted almost by committee and the extremely casual "How d'ye do, Colonel?" instead of a smart salute must have driven the poor man almost to the point of distraction.

Just over 85 years later on 4th February 1948, one could be excused if the inspection of the former Kent & East Sussex Light Railway by officials of the newly formed British Railways concluded a not dissimilar sentiment. To be fair, they cannot have expected miracles with Hitler's War only recently concluded on top of the financial uncertainties of the 1930s, but the outgoing management had nevertheless succeeded in presenting a reasonable engine in the form of Terrier No.3, the erstwhile "Bodiam", to head the Southern's Inspection Saloon. The staff were poorly paid and had no pension arrangements. The state of the signalling apparently left much to be desired, fencing, sidings and platforms were in poor condition, and tow-roping was in general use to facilitate shunting in sidings. However, the main technical hitch, apart from a general lack of serviceable stock, most of which rapidly disappeared for scrap, appears to have been the total absence of a Rule Book.

By rights; by the law of averages; by any rational point of view, let alone any vestige of common sense, the K&ESR in its entirety should have long ceased to exist. At best it should be a green access route/cycle path; at worst, melting back into the Wealden countryside whence it was born. Incredibly, whilst parts of the old route are both of these, almost half survives as a mainly steam operated Heritage Railway and there remains the challenge of how to close the missing link between Bodiam and Robertsbridge.

The town of Tenterden was initially bypassed to the north by the original South Eastern Railway, which took the line of least resistance, rather than following more direct and traditional transport corridors. Between 1842 and 1844, it was opened in stages from Redhill to Folkestone and Dover by way of Tonbridge and Ashford – both of which became important junctions. To the south-east of Tenterden, Hastings and Ashford were connected via Appledore for geographical and military reasons (1851), then finally, the town found itself marooned in a railway triangle, closed to the west by a line linking Tonbridge and Hastings (1852) by way of Tunbridge Wells (1845), Robertsbridge and Battle.

The history of efforts to remedy the situation, chiefly but not exclusively via Headcorn, would last to almost the end of the reign of Queen Victoria. Meanwhile, most of Tenterden's rival communities in the Kentish Weald – Hawkhurst and the old wool/weaving town of Cranbrook plus the villages of Horsmonden and Goudhurst were nominally joined to the national network by the Cranbrook & Paddock Wood Railway opened in 1892/3 that became better known as the Hawkhurst Branch.

Tenterden, a former limb of the Antient (sic) town of Rye – member of the famous Cinque Ports – finally acquired a railway in less than ideal circumstances. Whilst most moribund schemes had favoured a link with Headcorn in one shape or form, success ultimately came by way of the Rother Valley (Light) Railway. From Robertsbridge, the railroad, built to the standard gauge, initially followed the course of the (Eastern) Rother, crossed its floodplain and then joined a tributary, the Newmill Channel, as far as Tenterden.

Though authorised by its own Act of Parliament, the project immediately wrote its name into the record book as being the first to take advantage of the Light Railways Act of 1896. This allowed for some leniency in terms of construction and operation in an effort to enable construction in marginal economic areas. Ultimately in the face of road competition, but not assisted by the restrictions subsequently placed on railways because they were deemed a "common carrier", the Act was a flop but it did at least provide a mechanism for reopening parts of disused lines in the preservation era.

The Rother Valley Railway was built by the famous engineer Holman Fred Stephens, who became better known as Colonel Stephens through promotion in 1916 to rank of Lieutenant Colonel in the Royal Engineers, Territorial Force. He had earlier been resident engineer for the Cranbrook & Paddock Wood as well as constructing the Rye & Camber Tramway, which opened in 1895. He was appointed General Manager of the RVR in 1899 and the following year became its Managing Director. In time, he established a private empire of light and narrow gauge schemes which he ran from offices at 23 Salford Terrace in Tonbridge.

If there is one common thread that links all eras of the railway's history, it is under-capitalisation. In 1948 it was deemed imprudent to close the line immediately, so soon after nationalisation, and the cost of bringing the whole railway up to scratch was relatively huge, so British Railways dithered for a few years. Although skilfully engineered, mainly on small embankments above the flood plain, skirting around the edges of promontories, and, in the case of Wittersham Bank, going up and over to avoid a more significant cutting or diversion in order to attain the course of the Newmill, it was bedevilled by numerous bridges with severe weight restrictions. Most of these were no more than culverts although a 66-foot span was required to cross the Rother to the east of Northiam.

Initially, the permanent way of the Rother Valley comprised rails spiked directly onto sleepers and although the initial speed of 15mph was raised to the now more familiar 25mph for a light railway, this mattered little due to a second Achilles Heel that haunts the line to this day, and at the same time contributes to its immense character – level crossings. On quiet days, when crossing keepers are unavailable, there are inevitable delays whilst train crew operate the gates, giving a real sense of the leisurely stop-go-stop nature of the old railway.

Because it was constructed as economically as possible, and there was no blueprint on which to base decisions, the RVR was built far too light. Whilst the track would gradually be improved, the nemesis of crossings and culverts wouldn't go away cheaply and as there was no money, they wouldn't go away at all. More immediately, the existing rolling stock, as British Railways would also discover almost half a century later, wasn't up to the job and the two brand-spanking-new Hawthorn Leslie 2-4-0 tank engines, "Tenterden" and "Northiam", needed urgent back-up.

A loan of £500 from Barclays Bank helped secure an 0-6-0 tank locomotive from the London Brighton & South Coast Railway, No.70 "Poplar", of a class officially given the traffic designation A, but more commonly known as Terriers (1872-1880). These engines were coming to the end of their working lives, or more correctly for some, their first incarnation. The purchase would create yet another record in years to come, in terms of longevity of association, but at the time, the LB&SCR can scarcely have believed their luck. They relieved the RVR of £650 in exchange for a pup that had to all intents and purposes been written off, from an accountant's perspective, if nothing else, when placed on the Surplus List in 1897. It is fair to say that the engine had a reasonable degree of titivation at Brighton in May 1901 before delivery the following month. But compared to a scrap value of around £125 there is no question which party had the better deal.

But the performance of newly re-liveried, numbered and named engine must have stunned Stephens and the RVR. The ability of No.3 "Bodiam" in service to perform relatively Herculean tasks on literally a couple of lumps of coal and cup of water, coupled with the heady mix of a short-lived light railway mania, would induce further actions on the locomotive front which with hindsight can only be described as marginally successful, both in terms of quality and quantity, starting with an experimental railmotor in March 1905.

On a more tangible basis, the original railway had extended an extra one and a half miles up the now famous Tenterden Bank in 1903, renamed itself the Kent & East Sussex (Light) Railway in 1904 and essentially committed long-term financial suicide when finally reaching Headcorn in 1905, with the assistance of the South Eastern. These two extensions were built to a much higher standard, including chaired track, but with the exception of a short tunnel north of Tenterden St Michaels, still crossed all other public roads on the level.

The cocktail of speculation for further expansion led to the acquisition in May 1905 of another Hawthorn Leslie tank – No.4 "Hecate", a brand new 0-8-0 that to all intents and purposes was well off the light railway scale, certainly with regard to movements south of Rolvenden, as the original Tenterden had been renamed. The small engine stock was still apparently in need of further reinforcement, so the K&ESR went back to the Brighton for more.

In July 1903, the Isle of Wight Central Railway had rejected No.671 "Wapping" (1872), sibling of the erstwhile "Poplar" due to poor cylinders and firebox. It had previously been hired c.1900 for the construction of the Sheppey Light Railway (1901) also engineered by Stephens. He may well have been aware of the qualities of the class in his younger days whilst training in London, and it seems likely this is how he became more familiar with the class at close quarters. Whether there was some sort of sentimental attraction or the LB&SCR had one eye on the forthcoming motor train trials, the fact of the matter was that it was sold to the K&ESR for £700 in January 1905, the same sum as when rejected 18 months earlier by the IWCR! It was not delivered until June that year and one is left to draw one's own conclusions over the transaction, bearing in mind Barclays loaned another whopping £600; there certainly seems to have been an element of take it or leave it. "Wapping" therefore became K&ESR No.5 "Rolvenden" and started another renowned characteristic of the line: there would be very few years when there would be fewer than two Terriers on the railway, although occasions when two have been available for service have very much been the exception rather than the rule since reopening in 1974.

It seems that at least for the remainder of the Edwardian era, the Terriers were the preferred motive power. Their relative longevity in service on the K&ESR, as with other minor lines, was due to the light work involved compared to the intense suburban traffic on the South London and East London Lines for which they had been designed. There is a fallacious tendency to think that railways don't change much over the years and this is particularly untrue in the case of the K&ESR. Probably because of lack of company money, Stephens continued to acquire second-hand engines and stock; one imagines on the premise of squeezing the last possible ounce of use out of the purchases. Amongst these were two 0-6-0 Ilfracombe Goods tender engines, of London & Southern Western origin, built by Beyer Peacock, which were acquired in 1910 and 1914. These two locomotives usurped the two Terriers from some services. The final Stephens acquisition, also in 1914, was a Manning Wardle 0-6-0ST of 1876 vintage.

With the world plunged into the chaos of the Great War in 1914, the Stephens empire along with the rest of the network, was swept into Government control for the duration, although he continued to manage his railways. Eric Campbell Geddes was charged with the task of determining the structure of railways once direct governance ended. He concluded nationalisation was too big a step too soon and with typical British compromise promulgated an interim measure by creating the Big Four, leaving most minor railways out of the new arrangement. By the time Stephens formally got his railways back in 1921, the short-lived post-war boom was over and economic decline kicked in almost immediately as road competition grew, particularly in rural areas. Whilst the original Rother Valley section, at least on paper, still returned a small profit, the millstone of the Headcorn Extension was dragging the railway down by the head.

Desperate measures, including the inauguration of back-to-back rail mounted omnibuses, drastically reduced the need for steam traction, although there was a trade-off, requiring specific freight trains to cover the work previously executed by the use of mixed trains. A mixed train usually consisted of a single brake passenger coach marshalled with the wagons, and delays were horrendous with prolonged shunting as a consequence at intermediate stations, doing little to boost the meagre passenger traffic.

Another unusual feature of K&ESR for much of its life was for unduly complicated timetables compared to the actual level of service. Some services started from, or terminated at Tenterden Town, creating extra workings to and from Rolvenden, whilst through workings would often require a change of engines.

Three events then inflicted major change. The Wall Street Crash was followed by Stephens suffering a stroke in 1930, which seriously incapacitated him. Another stroke led to his demise at The Lord Warden Hotel, Dover on 23rd October 1931. Finally, three of the mainstays, an Ilfracombe Goods and both Terriers, clapped out about the same time, a situation unfortunately mirrored on other Colonel Stephens' lines, notably the Shropshire & Montgomeryshire. With the railway already popular amongst enthusiasts, Rolvenden specifically became a Mecca to witness rotting locomotives and rolling stock gradually disappearing into the undergrowth.

Stephens was succeeded by William H Austen, who had been his assistant ever since the construction of the Cranbrook & Paddock Wood. The economic situation coupled with growing international tensions meant this was no time for general railway closures, except in extreme cases, and besides, the geographical location of the line remained important.

1932 was a cataclysmic year in the history of the K&ESR. The Southern Railway forced the line into receivership, with Austen proposed as Receiver and Manager. The service was halved and use of the unpopular railbuses slashed, and photographic evidence suggests that the line had to rely disproportionately once more on its original Hawthorn Leslie tanks. However Austen eased the situation by disposing of "Hecate", and replacing it with an ex-London & South Western 0-6-0ST. This would provide worthwhile service until the next big clearout under British Railways auspices in 1948.

Two other major events occurred in the 1930s that were to have long-term ramifications to the present day. Parts from the two Terriers were combined with elements from at least one other from the Shropshire & Montgomeryshire Railway to create a reincarnation, given the No.3 without a name. Secondly, the railway started to hire locos from the Southern, due to the failings of the Hawthorn Leslie tanks and the second Ilfracombe Goods, in order to maintain the service. The first of these in 1936 was No.1556, a P-class 0-6-0 originally built by the South Eastern & Chatham in 1909, and happily still running on the railway to this day. But the hireling of choice would be the Terrier and the first of these was 2655, best known as "Stepney" on the Bluebell Railway. This process continued to kindle the flames of interest amongst enthusiasts and indeed is a direct antecedent of the hiring/swapping of engines on Heritage Railways in times of shortage or for marketing reasons.

No. 2 "Northiam" had one final hurrah, however, when it starred as "Gladstone" alongside Will Hay, Moore Marriott and William Moffatt in the timeless and incomparable 1937 Gainsborough classic "Oh Mr Porter!"

In the first winter of the war, the railway hired Terrier 2678; it was recorded in the Register as being in service from February 1940. This engine, fondly known by its old LB&SCR name of "Knowle", dated from the last batch constructed in 1880 having had a peripatetic existence for most of its life. It proved so successful that it stayed until 1958. Thankfully it too is now back on its old stamping ground and after a prolonged restoration, saw sterling service between 1999 and 2006.

On 26th March 1949 when working the 5.50pm from Robertsbridge, 32678 hauling a single coach was derailed between Northiam Station and the Rother Bridge. A month later she was recovered using cranes from Brighton and Bricklayers Arms. Damage was apparently relatively minor with the bunker coming off worst due to impact of the coach.

Traffic remained poor after the war so it was announced that the line would close to passenger traffic, and totally north of Tenterden Town, with effect from Monday 4th January 1954. The last train was run as an excursion on Saturday 2nd from Headcorn to Robertsbridge and back, and was worked Rolvenden-Robertsbridge-Rolvenden by 32678 and "Stepney", now 32655. The latter had been transferred to Ashford in May 1953 – Rolvenden was now only a sub-shed – and many of the photographs from this time feature the engine at work.

Freight traffic continued on the old Rother Valley section throughout the 1950s, augmented by seasonal Hop Pickers Specials as far as Bodiam until 1958. Three excursion trains were also run during this period, top and tailed by Terriers because of the weakness of bridges and culverts. Goods traffic continued to decline and as a consequence it was announced the line would close to all traffic from Monday 12th June 1961. The Hawkhurst branch was also scheduled for total closure at the same time; the Locomotive Club of Great Britain ran a final special on the Sunday, which incorporated both routes. Appropriately 32670, as the old No.3 had become under BR, was available to work the train at the Robertsbridge end whilst 32662, formerly "Martello" was making a very rare K&ES appearance at the Tenterden end. The seven coach train that they worked over the line must have been one of the heaviest ever worked by two Terriers, at least in peacetime.

History has a habit of repeating itself, and a minor mania erupted, albeit on a gentler scale, as enthusiasts and interested organisations and bodies sought to reopen disused railways that were progressively being closed; a process accelerated as a consequence of the Beeching Report. Some preliminary plans failed, like the old Westerham branch, which part-disappeared under tarmac – in that case the M25.

The K&ESR was too important in the history of our railways – too idiosyncratic, too eccentric, too loved – to be allowed to die. The story of those tortuous 13 years following closure has been covered in the railway's house magazine, *The Tenterden Terrier* and in Nick Pallant's book *Holding The Line*.

A compromise was eventually struck that allowed for the preservation of the Tenterden Town to Bodiam section, a distance of ten and a half miles. This still included five major road crossings, including the A28 twice, at Rolvenden and Northiam. There was a huge amount of work to do, as with the exception of the permanent way (which varied from poor to decrepit), most platforms – which in any case were far to short – the water tower at Rolvenden and the main station buildings at Tenterden, Northiam and Bodiam, there was quite literally nothing left.

Before the first part of the line reopened, a very special occasion was held at Rolvenden on 4th November 1972 when No.3 "Bodiam", as she had now reverted, celebrated her centenary, attracting a crowd reported to be around 2000, which today would be regarded as exceptional, let alone allowing for the time of year.

Public services recommenced on 3rd February 1974, initially running from Tenterden Town to just beyond Rolvenden. The first service was operated by the GWR railcar No.20 that at the time of writing is the subject of a major appeal to complete its prolonged rebuild. A Terrier, but sadly not "Bodiam", needless to say hauled the first steam train. Assigned the K&ESR No.10, another indication of the fierce pride in the line's independence, the former "Whitechapel", 32650, was purchased by the London Borough of Sutton for prospective display outside a new Civic Centre; there had been a Terrier called "Sutton", No.32661 but it had been cut up in 1963. The engine was loaned to the railway, and for much of its operational time faced the traditional direction of Robertsbridge unlike every other engine, except for short periods or special occasions.

As a charity – a not for profit organisation – it soon became apparent that train rides, even backed up by a souvenir shop and refreshment facilities, were never going to generate enough cash to get the existing railway up to scratch, let alone return trains to Bodiam. Enterprise spawned activities including long term success stories such as the "Wealden Pullman" and Santa Specials, innovations like cab rides, railway experience days, Fish & Chip Specials and Thomas the Tank Engine, plus the almost inevitable Galas, 1940s themes, and of course Hoppers' Weekend. Sadly though some events are now too expensive and risky to put on, especially the long-lamented Steam & Country Fairs.

Optimistic plans to reach Bodiam by 1980 proved hopelessly wide of the mark, but an early decision to raise the weight limit as resources allowed has more than paid dividends. Initially the workforce was totally voluntary, but help came in the form of various Job Creation Programme/Manpower Services Commission grants to help get people off the dole queues at a time of rapid inflation and increased unemployment.

In November 1976, thanks to a donation by Kent County Council, and the J.C.P., the feeble bridge over the Newmill Channel, three miles from Tenterden, was replaced by a much more substantial structure, enabling trains to reach Wittersham Road the following spring. The station also had to be totally rebuilt; employees under the J.C.P. scheme were also involved with the project.

By 1983 trains were running almost five miles, as permission had been granted to propel over Wittersham Bank out to Hexden Bridge, another tributary of the Rother. In order to raise money for further expansion, the railway issued bearer bonds, paying a fixed interest. The first of these in 1980 was a modest affair, but those of 1987 and 1998 contributed significantly towards the extensions to Northiam in 1990 and Bodiam in 2000.

The K&ESR also pulled off two significant coups in association with these two projects. In the case of Northiam, there was an enormous boost when a staged entry to the station was arranged in association with the famous "Challenge Anneka" TV programme. With regard to Bodiam, the railway secured a Millennium Commission grant that helped to deliver the project on time and in budget.

Effectively a splendid new railway was constructed westwards from Northiam on the foundation of the old with concrete sleepers, deep ballast, new rail and every other joint welded. Unfortunately, for the fortunes of the K&ES, the opening of the extension coincided with the worst in a series of financial crises. An appeal for cash had to be made to members, and like a century earlier, the line had to borrow money to keep afloat.

My first K&ESR classic. Slightly panned, I recorded Terrier No.10 "Sutton" (Whitechapel) piloting Austerity No.24 "William H Austen" out of Tenterden Town Station with a working to Wittersham Road during the superlative Steam & Country Fair of 16th/17th September 1978.

The timetable for the first season proved over-ambitious, and comparatively rarely for the preserved/heritage era, K&ESR also found themselves short of engines which made matters worse. Since 2000, the main service has stabilised at a train of usually Mark One coaches making three round trips a day from Tenterden Town, augmented by two trips with the celebrated Vintage Train, almost always drawn by the P-class or a Terrier, or the DMMU.

The heritage railway operating today is a far cry from the initial tentative service offered back in 1974 and it should be noted the Tenterden Railway Company/Kent & East Sussex Railway Co Ltd has now operated the line for more years than Colonel Stephens achieved. Key posts, where added value can be achieved, notably in engineering, catering, marketing and administration are now salaried, whilst volunteers carry out other tasks, including most of the actual operation of the trains.

Hugh Nightingale
Kingsnorth, Ashford, Kent
May 2008

BTH "Ford" Diesel works the Vintage Train into Northiam with the 12.14pm from Bodiam during the Diesel Weekend, 4th November 2006; the secondman preparing to give up the staff to the signalman. The train terminated in the Up Platform (the nominal No.2) in readiness to operate three Northiam-Bodiam-Northiam shuttles, the last of these working back to Tenterden Town.

The author is grateful to Mr Brian Janes for suggestions and minor alterations to the original script

The Millennium-Commission-supported scheme to reopen Northiam to Bodiam culminated successfully exactly one hundred years later to the day since the original Rother Valley Railway opened to passengers on 2nd April 1900. No.25 "Northiam" piloted by 32678 are seen working the train for VIPs and special guests back to Tenterden Town with Bodiam Castle in the background.

STEAM AT BODIAM

Almost a generation prior to the formal reopening, Bodiam saw some steam trains, in no small way thanks to the dedicated members of the Thameside Area Group led by the late George Wright. Although low-key affairs, they performed the essential function of publicising the ultimate goal as well as providing variety for members and enthusiasts.

Peckett 0-4-0T of 1923 No.12 "Marcia" is seen with (District) coach No.100 at the unrestored Bodiam Station on 31st August 1981. At the time of writing this attractive little engine is approaching the end of a long term rebuilding project, led by her owner Dick Beckett.

Former Dorking Greystone Lime Co No.3 "Baxter", built by Fletcher Jennings of Whitehaven in 1877, and a Bluebell resident since 1960, makes an absolutely charming scene amongst the trees and blossom-laden hedgerows surrounding the headshunt west of the station on 30th May 1983.

HOW D'YE DO COLONEL?

The Colonel is commemorated not only in an award-winning museum situated at present in a converted Nissen hut just to the north of Tenterden Town Station but also by having one of the railway's ex-Army 0-6-0ST Hunslet Austerity locomotives, named after him.

In the museum are displays of Light Railway ephemera featuring the tiny engine "Gazelle", originally from the Shropshire & Montgomeryshire and now on loan from the National Railway Museum. Included are many relics rescued from No.23 Salford Terrace in this re-creation of his office, although Stephens himself is an automated mannequin.

Without enhancement – the sky really was blue, No.23 "Holman F Stephens" storms up Tenterden Bank between the Wet Cutting and Cranbrook Road Level Crossing with the returning 11.30am Santa Special of 17th December 2006. It entered K&ESR service in August 1974, and with the exception of overhauls, has been a regular performer ever since.

No.24 is my favourite Austerity, simply by virtue of having featured more regularly in some of my better pictures than any other engine on the line. 3800 of 1953, it was originally called "William H Austen" for K&ESR service, after Stephens' assistant, but was renamed "Rolvenden" in 1995. With the Sunday Luncheon "Wealden Pullman" of 21st October 2007, she is seen working hard at the foot of Tenterden Bank.

The third Austerity currently in regular service is No.25 "Northiam" (3797 of 1953). The loco is seen putting up a brave face at the head of some troublesome trucks, rounding Orpin's Curve en route to Tenterden Town for a Day Out With Thomas ©™. Like the other two Hunslets, this loco has performed regularly since April 1982, when it was dedicated by TV personality Andrew Gardner.

STATIONS TO TENTERDEN TOWN

To start with I've chosen a few photographs illustrating the station areas on the railway in the Up direction from Bodiam to Tenterden Town. When the railway was built, Up was from Headcorn to Robertsbridge, but in preservation days, this was reversed and Up is now towards Tenterden Town. This is also more appropriate for the gradient of the Tenterden Bank.

Perennially in the National Trust top 20 of popularity by visitor numbers, the fairytale castle of Bodiam, more residence than fortification, is captured from the south-east on 17th October 1983. Even in Colonel Stephens' day it was eyed as a possible destination for passenger traffic on the railway. The castle, surrounded by its moat and picture-perfect setting was built by Sir Edward Dalyngrigge after 1385 thanks to marriage and his profitable campaigning in France.

Bodiam Station was skilfully remodelled to accommodate a five-coach platform and modern toilet facilities disguised as a coal office, whilst still being true to its light railway roots. Here we see the South Eastern & Chatham Railway P-class No.753, built at Ashford in 1909, departing for Tenterden Town with the 11.40am service during the Hop Pickers' Weekend, on the 12th September 2004.

Viewed from the other side of the track is the former London Brighton and South Coast Railway No.70 "Poplar", originally constructed at Brighton in 1872 but subject to several rebuilds since. By virtue of Terrier tradition, and its association with the line going back to 1901, RVR/K&ESR No.3 is most commonly referred to simply as "Bodiam". On a chilly 9th July 2006 she is seen at the head of the Vintage Train waiting departure; the run-round loop in the foreground was only a long siding in the old days worked by tow-rope.

21

753 has the distinction of being the first engine to be hired by the K&ESR from the Southern Railway on three occasions, 1936, 1938 and 1947 when it was numbered 1556 – appropriately the first livery in which it ran after restoration and re-entry to service. Running into the main platform at Northiam around 1pm, the Vintage train is passing the "Wealden Pullman", awaiting departure for Bodiam with a Sunday Luncheon service on 1st May 2005.

"Bodiam" seen leaving Northiam Station with the Vintage Train on the 9th April 2007 with the 12.45pm ex-Bodiam. The engine has had a chequered history on the line since returning to Robertsbridge on 10th April 1964, including a long period of dereliction.

The Terrier Trust was formed on the 16th September 1995 to secure the future of the locomotive in association with the then Tenterden Railway Company (now Kent & East Sussex Railway Company Ltd) who own and operate the line as a registered educational charity. A new boiler was fabricated by Israel Newton and the engine restored to service in the blue livery it would have first worn on the RVR.

23

"Bodiam" was scheduled to work on the post-Christmas/New Year 2008 trains, and following a planning error it was hoped to run a mini-charter from Tenterden Town to Wittersham Road and back on the morning of Saturday 29th December 2007. This was thrown into doubt by some relatively minor frost damage, so in the end it ran as empty coaching stock. Not being privy to any of the shenanigans it was only by the skin of my teeth and by pure chance I got down to the railway in time! The weather was impeccable for the time of year and with the Terrier at the head of the Vintage Train, I was able to record this stunning shot of the empties departing.

Opposite: When returned to service in SE&CR livery with its original number of 753, the engine was permitted to face south for a few years. This allowed the rarely photographed aspect of the west end of Wittersham Road to be recorded with a mixed train for Northiam and Bodiam on 13th April 2003. The station building, at right-angles to the track like the original, came from Borth near Aberystwyth whilst, totally appropriately for the P-class, the reconstructed Signal Box came from Deal Junction near Dover.

On closure of the line, 31556, as 753 was numbered in BR days, was purchased by James Hodson & Sons to work their mill at Robertsbridge, where it was named "Pride of Sussex". The stub of the old K&ESR was worked as a private siding for the rest of the decade, and when it closed, the engine was acquired for preservation. In this shot from the popular Visitors' Gallery, 753 runs from the Up Loop into the station at Rolvenden, having exchanged tokens with the signaller, working the 12.45pm from Bodiam on 11th June 2005.

Finally in this section, Austerity No.25 "Northiam" is seen from the platform storming up the Bank on the approach to Tenterden Town Station, with the 2.15pm from Bodiam on 4th November 2007. The weekend marked the launch of the line's "Rail Trails" pack, to encourage walks from, and between, stations on the line.

NORWEGIAN

The only resident tender engine on the K&ESR is "Norwegian", No.19, the former Norwegian State Railways No.376 – one of a batch of eight (like the P-class), built in Sweden in 1919. Very popular for Railway Experience Days, it is a useful and capable alternative on the Vintage Train, but limited to three bogie coaches on the main set due to its low axle weight. I find it difficult to photograph and it has unfortunately proved a nemesis on too many occasions over the years, so in some ways it is my least favourite locomotive.

Mid-week running in September 2005 saw 376 running with a rearranged main set strengthened by SE&CR four-wheeler 2947. On either the 21st or 22nd, the train was observed on the 11.40am from Bodiam on the approach to Cranbrook Road Level Crossing. The engine was withdrawn from service in October 2005 for a major overhaul.

Lesley Lee and Pete Hubbard sort out a problem with a hand lamp at Tenterden Town Station on 27th February 2005; 376 "Norwegian" stands in the loop. The engine is allocated No.19 in the K&ESR list.

A super shot of 376 posed on Orpin's Curve with the Vintage Train, with the 15.25pm from Bodiam during daily running in August 2005. It was taken from the balcony of the SR brake van in the infamous siding that unfortunately took out some of the best views of the line for both Up and Down trains, as witnessed in many photographs over the years. The guard had to operate the gates that day, hence the delay.

PANNIER

An interesting variation in the fleet is the only surviving Class 16XX Pannier 0-6-0PT presented in a pseudo-GWR livery, formerly on the South Devon Railway. Although a product of Swindon to an F W Hawkworth design, it is actually a BR engine of 1951 making it a near contemporary of the Austerities.

Since the line reopened to Bodiam, this pleasant location on Orpin's Curve between the Occupation Crossing and the foot of the Bank proper is one place one does not need bright sunshine due to the relative lateness of the first Up train. Slightly spoilt by having the cylinder cocks open which marginally take out the marker oak tree to the right of shot, 1638 heads the Victorian Train with the 11.43am Rolvenden to Tenterden Town on 28 March 2004 during the 50th anniversary of closure weekend.

Around Cranbrook Road Level Crossing on a clear evening it is just possible to have the light on a train from the north around Midsummer's Day. On Saturday 3rd June 2006, 1638 works the "Wealden Pullman" downhill below the crossing; the buttercups and hedgerow in the foreground bathed in the warm sunshine.

This enchanting scene of 1638 on the 1.50pm from Bodiam on 3rd May 2008 arriving at Tenterden Town Station during the Gala shows that even on fine days, provided there is enough cloud to eradicate the heaviest of shadows, worthwhile pictures can be obtained looking into the light. The sun illuminates the spectators and bluebells effectively yet detail is still retained on the front of the smokebox.

BLACK MAGIC BOX

One of the famous Terrier locomotives, 32678 was built at Brighton in 1880 being one of the final eight. It has the distinction of being the only surviving working member from the batch and was the second A1 to be rebuilt as an A1X in 1911. A peripatetic engine to say the least for most of its career, its finest hour came when transferred to the K&ESR early in 1940, playing an important role during and after the war. Purchased after withdrawal for display at Butlin's, Minehead, it is now wholly owned by The Terrier Trust.

When returned to service on 30th May 1999, dedicated by editor and personality Ian Hislop, "Knowle" was turned out as Southern 2678, the guise it wore when first hired to the K&ESR in 1940. Thanks to the hospitality of Mark Yonge I was able to use his garden as a hide; the sheep not at all bothered by the train, just below Cranbrook Road crossing on 9th January 2000.

Wednesday 29th June 2005 was a very hot midsummer's day, which not only featured the Vintage Train, but it also ran the first service of the day. Whilst not normally associated with being ideal conditions for photography, it afforded the front of the smokebox to be in direct sun and no shadow from the canopy at Bodiam on the carriages themselves. 32678 is seen departing with the 11.40am working.

On Sunday 22nd May 2005, having been trapped in the shed at Rolvenden earlier in the season, no thanks to a family of black-birds nesting in "Norwegian", the Terrier makes a classic departure from Northiam with the 12.45pm from Bodiam. Previously advertised as the Victorian Train, the inclusion of the Woolwich coach of 1911 caused a rebranding to Vintage Train. Even so, I think this vehicle looks particularly attractive coupled next to the Terrier.

Above: Following he visit to the Mid-Hants Railway in 2004, 32678 was off-loaded the wrong way round, so it ran facing Robertsbridge for the weekend event marking the 50th anniversary of passenger closure, celebrated in March. Unfortunately for my day off on Sunday 28th, the weather proved rather uncooperative, especially for 32678 working a short freight, 1.00pm from Tenterden Town to Rolvenden, at the favoured location on the Bank with St Mildred's in the background.

Right: A view of the cab of 32678 photographed at Tenterden Town on 18th March 2006. Notice the floor-level firebox door, necessitating a contortionist ability on behalf of the fireman.

HEY, HEY, USAs!

The two USA 0-6-0T locomotives have been popular performers over the years. Unfortunately, they have a tendency to waddle due to their outside cylinders and short wheelbase. They were built to the design of Colonel Howard G Hill at the Vulcan Ironworks in Pittsburgh, PA in 1943 for service overseas. The Southern Railway purchased 14 after the war for shunting services in Southampton Docks. Now numbered 21 and 22 in the K&ESR listing, they are owned by the K&ESR Locomotive Trust.

No.21 as DS238 "Wainwright" waits in the platform at Bodiam Station with the 12.19pm to Tenterden Town on 26th May 2003. Restoration commenced on this engine in 1988, having undergone a boiler swap with No.22 in 1978, and it entered service in 1994 with the departmental stock number and name acquired in 1963.

I remain very fond of this delightful scene at Rolvenden, now essentially eliminated by development of the adjacent Rother Valley Timber, which occupies the site of the old engine shed and yard. Newly returned to service after an overhaul, No.22 "Maunsell" arrives at Rolvenden with a train from Wittersham Road on Easter Monday, 20th April 1981.

If I recall correctly, I have Dave Brailsford to thank indirectly for arranging for this wonderful and very special juxtaposition of the two USAs at Northiam Station on 21st June 1997. No.22 had just been restored to service in Southern livery as No.65 having previously worked as No.22 and BR 30065.

A rare outing for my Yashica-G 6x6 and the combination of brilliantly clear autumn conditions with a fairly low mid-day sun without the inconvenience of long shadows. This resulted in a splendid portrait of WD1960 "Wainwright" standing in the Up Platform (Platform 2) waiting to depart for Bodiam with the "Wealden Pullman" on 16th October 2005.

DIESELS

Some people like diesels whilst others do not. I am firmly of the opinion that as the railway is an Educational Charity, quite apart from the economics, diesels are very much part of the set-up. Indeed, with locomotive-hauled passenger trains all but eradicated from the national network, they have an important part to play, quite apart from their "Thunderbird" role.

Class 33 'Crompton' No. D6570 "Ashford", built at BRCW (Birmingham Railway Carriage and Wagon) in 1961, is viewed with passenger stock in the loop at Tenterden Town during a shunting manoeuvre in the weak late afternoon sunshine of Saturday 8th October 2005.

Class 14 No.14029, K&ESR No.49, passes the BTH (British Thomson Houston) "Ford" Diesel of 1932, at Northiam in cold wet weather during an uncommon Diesel Weekend, 10th – 11th March 2001. The latter was one of three diesel-electrics built for the car plant at Dagenham, Essex.

Class 08 No. D3174 "Dover Castle", constructed at Derby in 1955, rounds Orpin's Curve on the approach to Rolvenden in bright sunshine with the 11.30am freight from Tenterden Town on 28th March 2004, marking fifty years since the railway closed to passengers. Normally restricted to shunting and short distance journeys it has worked the occasional passenger train in emergencies, including the "Wealden Pullman".

W20W, conveniently No.20 in the K&ESR listing, is an AEC-powered railcar built by the GWR at Swindon; the first of a batch of 15, it entered service on 4th June 1940. Earlier models with a more rounded outline had led to the acquisition of their nickname of "Flying Banana". It formed the very first public paying train on 3rd February 1974 and for the rest of the decade worked November and Saturday morning trains. The subject of a long restoration task I was fortunate to ride on it once and thus able to obtain this splendid shot at Wittersham Road, including the redoubtable Howard Ashton. The scene dates from Easter 1979 and is thus probably the 11.45am from Tenterden Town on Saturday 14th April.

CLASS 108 DMMU

The railway is fortunate to have use of a ubiquitous Class 108 DMMU (Diesel Mechanical Multiple Unit) two car set, commonly referred to as Derby Lightweight. It is totally in the Light Railway tradition; such units being regarded as a direct descendant of the GWR railcars and of course the original back-to-back railbuses.

With the bluebells in their prime, the 108 seen leaving Tenterden Town forming the 2.20pm service on Thursday 4th May 2006. The set has literally proved its weight in gold since the reopening to Bodiam in 2000, enabling an additional two return trips to be run on days when visitor numbers do not justify a second steam locomotive.

Freshly repainted and part-framed by a wonderful overhanging willow, the 108 is viewed approaching the Rother Bridge with the 11.45am Tenterden Town to Bodiam on 11th May 2008.

ABSENT FRIENDS

There have been several goings as well as comings over the years, but for reasons of space and topicality, just two are featured in this book.

Most lamented of all, inevitably, is the Terrier that was formerly designated No.10 "Sutton". It was actually LB&SCR No.50 "Whitechapel" and has one of, if not the most interesting histories of all the Terriers, arriving at Robertsbridge in September 1964. Although it never ran on the K&ESR prior to this date, and therefore not really a 'K&ESR-Terrier' in the strictest interpretation, it proved an absolute 'brick' until its cylinders gave up the ghost in 1994. Now slowly being restored on the Spa Valley Railway, Tunbridge Wells, it is seen here in happier times steaming out of Tenterden Town Station in the gorgeous summer sunshine of 21st July 1985 with the 1.20pm to Hexden Bridge.

An immensely successful and enjoyable adjunct to the Thameside Area Group's events organised at Bodiam in the early 1980s was the utilisation of the A.C.Cars Railbus W79978. This was based at Tenterden from 1980 to 1984, replacing the GWR Railcar on quieter services. It also proved ideal as an attraction running more than two miles from Bodiam back towards Northiam to a specially created rural halt bordering the Great Dixter Estate where this photograph was obtained on 25th May 1981.

VISITORS

The costing of hiring alternative motive power is as dubious and as subjective as the costing of railways themselves. Whatever the arguments for and against, the process does at least provide variety and allows people to have the opportunity to see different types of motive power than would otherwise be the case. The process of swapped-steamings helps to reduce costs and enables K&ESR engines to travel to other lines as well.

Above: The then almost new replica of "Rocket" and (Famous) "Fenchurch", the first of the Terriers to enter service in 1872 and now resident on Bluebell, are seen especially lined-up for the press at Tenterden Town on 15th September 1981.

Opposite: The late George Wright on the footplate of "Rocket" just to the north of the platform at Tenterden Town so the tower of St Mildred's Parish Church may be included in the background. 15th September 1981.

USA No.22 "Maunsell" piloted by "Fenchurch" make a storming ascent of Tenterden Bank just below Cranbrook Road crossing during the Steam & Country Fair Weekend on 19th September 1981 – probably the 1.10pm ex-Wittersham Road.

Keighley & Worth Valley Railway stalwart Ivatt Class 2MT 2-6-2T No. 41241, built at Crewe in 1949, paid a very brief visit over New Year 1982-83 following an overhaul by Resco (Railways) at Woolwich. Its only public runs, subject to speed restraints on Tenterden Bank, were on Sunday 2nd January. It is seen emerging from the mist, light engine, just outside Rolvenden, bound for Tenterden Town. The old hop-poles (left of centre) lasted for many years and feature in many older photographs taken in this area.

I tried several long-focus views from Mounts Lane in the early years, and this one, more or less forced because of the sheer numbers of photographers elsewhere, is undoubtedly one of my all time favourites. It shows 41241 about three-quarters of a mile outside Rolvenden descending Pope's Bank past the Morghew Estate, with the 2.15pm Wittersham Road to Tenterden Town on 2nd January 1983. The five-coach train in K&ES brown & cream, the very similar Pullman livery of "Barbara" and a fairly large engine helped make this mid-winter scene from a distance; a similar opportunity has never presented itself since!

The most popular "new" visitor ever, in my opinion, was the Severn Valley-based Ivatt Class 2MT 'Mogul' (2-6-0) 46443 built at Crewe in 1950. It stayed for six weeks in 1995 and although the actual 21st Anniversary celebrations in June were rather spoilt by the weather, I was able to take this classic departure scene from Northiam on Sunday 14th May with the 11.45am for Tenterden Town.

Curiously, like the Terriers, 10 LMS Fowler 3F 0-6-0T "Jinty" engines have survived. Visiting from the Keighley & Worth Valley in the summer of 1997 was 47297 from a batch of 20 constructed by the Vulcan Foundry in 1924. With a classic K&ES mixed train, the engine leaves Northiam for Tenterden Town with the 11.20am service on 14th September.

51

A second guest from the Keighley & Worth Valley Railway was 0-6-0 Well Tank "Bellerophon", built by the Haydock Foundry for the Haydock Collieries in 1874 and now owned by the Vintage Carriages Trust. Unusually for the preservation/heritage era, it faced south. With Chris Mitchell on the footplate it is viewed entering Northiam with the 12.15pm from Tenterden Town on Sunday 20th July 1997.

Another 3F 0-6-0T "Jinty", No. 47298 from the Llangollen Railway, was of particular interest because, like the resident Austerities, it was actually built by Hunslet in Leeds. Dating from November 1924, it is seen storming up Tenterden Bank just below Cranbrook Road crossing. It had been hired in at short notice to cover the 1998 Santa Specials; this picture was taken on New Year's Day 1999.

Possibly the most fascinating visitor has been the 1987-built replica of the 1828 pioneer French locomotive "Marc Seguin", seen at Tenterden Town on Saturday 17th July 1999 during the 25th Anniversary Celebrations. The replica "Rocket" also attended for a second time.

A very popular engine in action during the summer of 2006 from the North Yorkshire Moors Railway was the Lambton tank No.29, seen on the Through Road at Wittersham Road, with the 2.15pm from Bodiam on 14th August. Note the very unusual Down Starting signal in the platform road.

For the Colonel Stephens-themed Gala in May 2007, former Great Eastern Railway (GER) J15 of 1912, built Stratford Works, and painted in its BR guise of 65462, was selected to make an inaugural visit; part of the reason being its similarity to the erstwhile Ilfracombe Goods engines. On Wednesday 2nd May it had a trial steaming after which it is seen resting in the Up Loop at Rolvenden in glorious late afternoon sunshine.

A1X Terrier No. W8 "Freshwater" is gently brought onto goods stock by Mick Harman in the platform road at Wittersham late on the afternoon of Saturday 5th May 2007; the goods stock was to be removed from the 5.43pm ex-Bodiam mixed train during the Colonel Stephens' Gala, and then shunted to sidings. Incredibly, this engine, based on the Isle of Wight Steam Railway, had never been to the K&ESR before! It was originally No.46 "Newington" and has had a most colourful career.

Former London suburban tank engines made an unusual straight swap in March 2008. Beyer Peacock Beattie 2-4-0 Well Tank as BR 30587 built for the London & South Western at Gorton, Manchester in 1874 and now based on the Bodmin & Wenford Railway is seen in the Up Platform at Northiam, with the Vintage Train, working the 12.13pm ex-Bodiam, 15th March, during the Branch Line Weekend. The following week "Bodiam" went to Cornwall, joining the Well Tank on the B&WR for Easter; possibly the first time a Terrier has ever visited the Duchy.

For the ambitious May Gala of 3rd – 5th May 2008, the railway welcomed two debut engines. Also from the Bodmin and Wenford Railway was 4575-class GWR Small Prairie 2-6-2T No.5552, completed at Swindon Works in November 1928. Seeing this superb engine coming off Willows Curve, half a mile south of Rolvenden, on the 4.05pm from Bodiam of 3rd May, it is impossible to comprehend that it spent 25 years of its life rotting it the Woodham's Yard at Barry!

The second Gala visitor, also making its debut, was the Class N7 69621 0-6-2T to an A J Hill design, formerly 999E then LNER 7999. It is based the North Norfolk Railway, and owned by the East Anglian Railway Museum and was the last of these GER engines to be completed, at Stratford Works in 1924. She is seen working the 12.30pm from Bodiam on the approach to Northiam on 5th May.

AROUND TENTERDEN TOWN

As the main station on the railway proper since 1903, many of the special events are centred in and around the station with all public passenger trains originating and terminating here.

An absolutely timeless general view of a deserted Tenterden Town Station at lunchtime on 16th October 1983. A solitary photographer records No.22 "Maunsell" running round on the level crossing and the stock of the mixed train stands by the platform, with milk churns that will never be dispatched or collected.

Not the sort of picture I would have gone out of my way to obtain, but in spite of the cold and wet conditions, quite an attractive scene in its own right with plenty of atmosphere. No.14 "Charwelton" had been hired for the filming of a "Jim'll Fix It" featuring the actor Nigel Havers as a Great War veteran returning home to his sweetheart. 19th April 1983.

A very rare and delightful cameo in the sidings in the warm sunshine of 30th August 1982 sees the Bluebell's Fletcher Jennings 0-4-0T "Baxter" bunker-to-bunker with the even smaller Peckett 0-4-0T No.12 "Marcia". The challenge facing owners and railways with such limited haulage capacity, even if vacuum fitted, is finding sufficient worthwhile work to justify the cost and time of restoration. Notwithstanding this fact, they are still an important part of our railway heritage and should be cherished as such.

753 stands in the loop at the head of the Vintage Train mid-morning on 16th March 2003, ready to play its part in the special event to mark the centenary of the station and the extension from Rolvenden (the original Tenterden).

Another general view of the station this time sees Class 33 D6570 "Ashford" running round in the soft autumnal light of 8th October 2005.

I'm not very good at disciplining myself in taking straightforward safe shots at what may be regarded as standard locations when the opportunity arises. This is an example of an exception. 32678 runs round on the level crossing; its beauty due to the uncluttered simplicity in A1 conditions, if not even A1X (!), on 2nd September 2005.

Another view of the Terrier W8 "Freshwater", this time in the loop on 7th May 2007. This engine has a pedigree of association with railways on the Isle of Wight almost as solid of that of "Bodiam" with the K&ESR. Readily apparent in this picture are three island hallmarks: retention of the raised sandboxes over the leading wheels, the extended bunker and the front footstep(s) for ease of access to the smokebox end of the engine. This latter feature has now been incorporated on both "Knowle" and "Bodiam".

Making the best of the prevailing weather conditions, this time for an alternative shot from the north side of the level crossing, "Bodiam" leaves with the 1.00pm to Bodiam on 1st January 2008

2005 SANTA SPECIALS

The Santa Special season during Advent 2005 was more than just a prelude to an amazing six-month period on the railway. From memory the 3rd wasn't that brilliant weather wise until late in the day so I didn't go down until the 4th, which started dull but then changed to lovely December sunshine, initiating fine conditions for most of the rest of the Santas. On average you might get one or two clear days during the whole period of operation so it was a bit like being a child let loose in a sweet shop...

The climb of Tenterden Bank of the 11.30am Santa Special, 18th December. 753 and 32678 working hard, between the Wet Cutting and Cranbrook Road Level Crossing backed by a beautiful blue sky. I was tempted to take the vapour trail out but decided against it as it makes the vivid sky seem less contrived.

A dramatic scene indeed! No.24 "Rolvenden" charges over Orpin's Occupation Crossing, all guns blazing, shortly after leaving Rolvenden with the returning 2.30pm Santa Special of 10th December. The irritating overhead cable at this location has been removed as particularly in this shot it would have distracted attention from the exhaust.

At Cranbrook Road Level Crossing, 32678 pilots 753 on the back working of the 12.15pm Santa Special of 11th December. There have been very few occasions when I have regretted missed opportunities, always being grateful for what I have, but this was one time I wished I had not been on nights and therefore failed to see the same combination 90 minutes earlier.

My regrets of 11th December were exacerbated by the events surrounding the Hemel Hempstead oil explosion and fire. The encroaching cloud and pollution in the atmosphere combined to create a most eerie light when, having swapped round, 753 and 32678 were again seen at Cranbrook Road crossing with the returning 1.45pm train.

BRITISH STEAM RAILWAYS

The next event in this historic series of happenings occurred on Wednesday 4th January 2006 for the filming of 32678 with a mixed train including the Woolwich coach and SE&CR No.2947 for the part-works series 'British Steam Railways' by Planet Three Publishing Network for De Agostini UK. They started filming in dark, damp and windy conditions, but then the cold front cleared...

Immediately after the sun came out, 32678 is seen working extra hard for the benefit of the cameramen up the Bank, between the Rolvenden Down Home Signal and the Wet Cutting.

Not working quite so hard and with perhaps a little too much steam coming from underneath the engine to be desirable, 32678 still makes a fine sight working uphill with the delightful High Weald countryside in the background.

With the January sun already starting to dip noticeably, this proved to be my best picture of the day's events of the whole train, approaching the shallow cutting between Cranbrook Road crossing and the Tenterden Town Home Signal.

72

'Some People Wait A Lifetime…' About 2.30pm the film crew decided to return to Tenterden Town for some shots at sundown in and around the station rather than round Orpin's Curve as suggested. I was unaware they also wanted some more views from the footplate; as a consequence they had to cut one of their sequences slightly short on the final DVD. My concern that there might be too much flare at this time in the afternoon proved unfounded, as the result proves.

ALL TERRIERS GREAT AND SMALL

The idea of ATGAS whelped from a proposal to have a visiting Terrier to mark the completion of the rebuild of No.3 "Bodiam" and eventually mushroomed to include all five available working Terriers. The two-day event was held on 6th and 7th May 2006 and included a display of 00 and 5-inch gauge Terriers as well as a dog show on the Sunday.

Bluebell allowed "Stepney" to visit for the first time in the preservation era provided it was kept to light duties; it was also permitted to face Robertsbridge. One of the Terriers originally based at New Cross, it achieved fame on the K&ESR as being the first Terrier to be hired from the Southern in 1938 and working part of the last passenger train with "Knowle" on 2nd January 1954. As the Bluebell's first engine and the subject of a Reverend Awdry book it has perhaps earned a disproportionate degree of fame compared to some of its kennel-mates. On Friday 5th May it was given a trial by running it on a Railway Experience Day and is seen working with the Woolwich coach in the station at Rolvenden.

After very dark and then wet conditions on the Saturday, the weather abated somewhat on Sunday. No.3 "Bodiam" is seen on-shed at Rolvenden early in the morning with "Martello"; the two famously worked the last passenger excursion organised by the Locomotive Club of Great Britain over the line on 11th June 1961.

Regarded as being a particularly good machine, LB&SCR No.62 "Martello", like "Stepney", was also making its preservation debut at Tenterden during ATGAS. Turned out with its duplicate list number of 662 in Marsh Umber, the engine is seen in the yard at Rolvenden in the weak morning sunshine of 7th May.

Although heavily involved with the event which rather limited photographic opportunities, I then had time to go to Wittersham Road where I was uniquely able to capture this delightful scene of 32678, suitably adjudged "Best of Breed", standing in the Through Road with the 9.28am freight to Tenterden Town.

"Fenchurch" with its pseudo number of 672 then joined 32678 at Rolvenden with a strengthening of the freight. The two engines then stayed together to work the 10.48 departure from Tenterden Town and with "Stepney" in the loop, presented an opportunity to record both Bluebell Terriers side by side in the station.

BRIGHTON WORKS CHARTER

To mark the return of "Stepney" to the K&ESR, a Photographic Charter was organised on Monday 8th May by Geoff Silcock of Sentimental Journeys to help pay transportation costs. It was decorated as former 'Brighton Works' ("Morden") with the BR number it carried shortly before withdrawal of 32635. The weather in the morning was as foul as it had been on Saturday afternoon but thankfully it took a turn for the better after lunch.

Photographic Charters provide many more opportunities than presented on a public day and make access to more remote areas much easier than would normally be the case. Track enhancements in recent years are evident in this scene at the Home Signal for Wittersham Road during a staged run-past.

This typical K&ESR scene is captured on the final approach to Bodiam Station; the sign for the footpath crossing the line linking Bodiam and Ewhurst Green may be seen in the background. The quality and effort that went into the Millennium Project is readily notice-able with concrete sleepers on a considerable bed of ballast.

It can be fairly easily to miss the obvious in station areas during charters and although not quite ideally posed relative to the Stop board protecting the level crossing, "Stepney" as 'Brighton Works' makes a fine sight in the late after-noon sunshine; you can just imagine it setting off for Robertsbridge some three and a half miles away. The train was just about to do a run-past at the west end of the station so I had to quickly get out of the way.

In my view a real gem, and an exceptionally rare opportunity to photograph an Up train at Northiam from the Newenden side of the crossing. There is probably too much flare to be ideal and a delay would have been preferred but there was the busy A28 to consider and most participants wanted a final flourish at Hexden Channel before sunset, which incidentally provided many of the published pictures of the event.

"BODIAM" CHARTER

The following day, the mixed train was rearranged with alternative stock to run with "Bodiam" to mark its return to action after 20 years on the sidelines. Members of The Terrier Trust had voted by a substantial margin to have the engine outshopped in Rother Valley Blue as K&ESR No.3 with nameplates. Again the weather started poorly but provided the memorable sight of both Terriers shunting at Rolvenden as 32678 was required for Railway Experience Day duty.

At Northiam the opportunity was taken to have several run-pasts into the station; the red 'Pegg' and 'Huxford' wagons proving an inspired choice in the rather murky conditions. The coach used was the former Great Eastern brake No.197; to the left is the Up Inner Home signal.

Blowing off furiously, "Bodiam" and the mixed train make a fine sight with the castle in the background; the sun cooperating at the right moment by poking out between the clouds. About a mile from Bodiam, this is one of, if not the most famous views of the railway and castle, but it should be noted it is taken from an access track on private property.

Some of the nicer views of trains can be obtained in and around Wittersham Road Station from late afternoon onwards, particularly on special days or charters. "Bodiam" is seen with the mixed train working down Wittersham Bank, from the level crossing, in the soft evening sunshine.

On the way back to Rolvenden, the opportunity was taken for a couple of run-pasts at Gazedown Wood. This used to be a very popular spot for dedicated railway photographers such as Brian Stephenson and Mike Esau, but it much less frequented in recent years, particularly with the introduction of the DMMU and alternative locations that do not require track access. The area as a whole has also become very overgrown since the cessation of the adjacent crayfish business but nevertheless this timeless picture makes for interesting comparison with the shot taken of the same engine as 32670 in the later section *Indian Summer*. See page 97.

THE WEALDEN PULLMAN

*An important part of the set-up on the Kent & East Sussex is the prestigious "Wealden Pullman"
providing mainly Saturday evening and Sunday lunchtime dining trains. It is also available
for private hire for functions such as business use or wedding receptions.*

Flagship of the "Wealden Pullman" is "Barbara", seen here in the Up (No.2) Platform at Northiam in the formation of a Sunday Luncheon service, coupled to 1638, on its outrun to Bodiam on 1st May 2005. Greater operational flexibility has been achieved by having this service originating and terminating at Northiam with the trade-off of two extra empty coaching stock workings from and to Tenterden Town.

A very unusual opportunity presented itself with the last running of the Sunday Luncheon "Wealden Pullman" of the 2004 season on 31st October, the day after the clocks went back. The weather was not uncommonly brilliantly clear for the time of year and the train was doubleheaded by Class 33 D6570 "Ashford" piloted by 753, which was still facing Robertsbridge at the time. The low sun lights the train almost straight on as it enters Wittersham Road bound for Northiam, making visibility tricky for the crew.

Another Sunday Luncheon "Wealden Pullman", drawn by WD1960 "Wainwright", is seen leaving Northiam for Bodiam shortly after 1.00pm on 16th October 2005. It includes both the former Hastings line Restriction '0' Pullman coaches, "Barbara" and "Theodora", flanking Restaurant Unclassified "Diana". "Theodora" served for many years as the station buffet at Tenterden Town and had the distinction of forming part of the last excursion over the line organised by the Locomotive Club of Great Britain on 11th June 1961 that was worked by "Bodiam" and "Martello".

BRIDGES

There are three watercourses of significance crossed by the railway: Newmill Bridge about a mile NNE of Wittersham Road Station; Hexden Bridge a slightly shorter distance to the SW of the same station, and the 66-foot Rother Bridge just under a mile ENE of Northiam Station.
Only the latter is accessible by public right of way.

When Gerald Siviour found out about this book project, he asked if I was going to include a picture of GWR Class 57XX 0-6-0PT (Pannier Tank) No.7752 that visited from Tyseley in 1986. So, killing two birds with one stone, here is the locomotive with the 3.48pm from Hexden Bridge to Tenterden Town on 24th August 1986 crossing Newmill Bridge.

Above: "Stepney" as 'Brighton Works' No.32635 posed on Hexden Bridge with its mixed train during Geoff Silcock's Sentimental Journeys Charter of 8th May 2006.

Opposite: Another view of the BTH "Ford" Diesel, working over Hexden Bridge at the head of the Vintage Train in perfect weather, with the 11.05am Tenterden Town to Bodiam during the Diesel Weekend on 4th November 2006.

Class 108 DMMU crosses the Rother Bridge bound for Bodiam, watched by Robbie from the Beckley (south) side, with the 11.45 from Tenterden Town on Sunday 23rd June 2002.

10 to 15 minutes earlier, "Norwegian" on the Rother Bridge with the 11.39 ex-Bodiam from the Newenden (north) side. It would have passed the DMMU seen in the other picture at Wittersham Road. 23rd June 2002.

No.23 "Holman F Stephens" works over the Rother Bridge with the 2.30pm Tenterden Town to Bodiam on 5th May 2008.

BUNKER AND TENDER FIRST

As a Light Railway, there has never been a turntable on the line, so unless double-headed bunker-to-bunker, a bunker (or tender) will lead one way. This does not mean that such journeys are not worth photographing; tank engines were specifically designed to go just as well backwards as forwards.

Classic K&ESR. No.10 "Sutton" (Whitechapel), was, if I remember rightly, having cylinder problems, limiting it to one coach. Correctly facing the traditional direction of Robertsbridge, the fireman receives the 'right-away' from the guard with the 1542 ex-Hexden Bridge for Tenterden Town on 15th July 1984.

376 "Norwegian" is seen from just off the A28 at Northiam, passing the Down Inner Home with the Vintage Train, or more correctly Victorian Train as the Woolwich coach did not enter service until 2004. Easter Sunday, 23rd April 2000.

"Bodiam" on arrival at Wittersham Road with the Vintage Train on 29th December 2007. In quite beautiful winter's sunshine, this view shows the main distinguishing feature of the engine: the unique raised bunker, topped with open coal rails. This was intended as a fairly cheap way of increasing the coal capacity and dates from the early 1930s' rebuild. The engine looks just right coupled to the SE&CR Saloon.

INDIAN SUMMER

The 17 months from August 1984 to December 1985 go down in K&ESR history as a rare spell of having two Terriers available for service at the same time. Not only that, but the weather was pretty special too; both years featuring sunny summers and blissful autumns…

On the 20th October 1984, near milepost 2 (from Tenterden), at the south end of Sewage Works straight, No.10 "Sutton" (Whitechapel) and "Bodiam" as 32670, double-head a mixed train on the 1.45pm ex-Tenterden Town. Note the oast house at Cold Harbour Farm in the background.

One problem photographing Terriers with Mark One or similar bogie stock is that the tiny engine can be almost lost against the black end of the vehicle. No such difficulty presented itself in crystal-clear sunshine on 10th November 1985 with "Bodiam" as 32670 working the 2.33pm from Hexden Bridge past Gazedown Wood. Oh for the same conditions with a three-coach 'birdcage' set in early BR red rather than K&ESR liveried Mark Ones!

You can almost sense the intensity of the frost as K&ESR No.3 "Bodiam" and No.22 "Maunsell", as 32670 and 30065, climb Tenterden Bank – again just below Cranbrook Road crossing – with the returning 2.00pm working of 30th December 1985. The oast is that of Isemonger, about a third of a mile from Cold Harbour, but almost a mile and a half separates this from that on page 96, indicative of the sinuous nature of this part of the line.

AMONGST THE GOLDEN DAFFODILS
Some photographers like glints, reflections or silhouettes when it comes to trains,
but for me nothing beats a swathe of golden daffodils, whatever the weather.

On the occasion of the centenary of the extension from the old Tenterden to Tenterden Town, 753 leaves the principal station with the 1.35pm service for Rolvenden on 16th March 2003.

Although the weather of St George's Day 2006 was nothing to get excited about, the late narcissi in bloom provided enough colour to complement this view of No.24 "Rolvenden", with Paul Beale on the footplate, departing Tenterden Town Station working the "Wealden Pullman". The signal box was originally based at Chilham, on the line from Ashford to Ramsgate via Canterbury West.

On March 28th 2004, the BTH "Ford" Diesel slowly works its way into Tenterden Town with the 1.37pm freight working from Rolvenden.

32678 departs Tenterden Town Station at 2.15pm with the Vintage Train on 28th March 2004, the weekend chosen to mark the 50th anniversary of closure to passenger traffic and the northern extension.

1638 on the level crossing at Tenterden Town Station with the 11.40am ex-Bodiam on 18th March 2007.

SNOWTIME

Everybody's favourite weather for photography, whatever the subject and more especially, where it is rare. The combination of steam and snow is quite tricky and the challenge is to get the best possibly results whilst minimising the risks.

1638 was used in the snowy conditions of New Year's Day 1997. Kent, like Cornwall, and indeed many other parts of the country, is renowned for its microclimates and variations, being three-quarters surrounded by water. Although cold, there was only a light covering of the white stuff around Tenterden with the roads reasonably passable. In Northiam it was a different story; the roads were icier with more snow. Even so it was a surprise to find the points at the level crossing end well and truly frozen solid. The few passengers and engine crew wait patiently in the bitter cold for them to be cleared whilst the north-easterly blows in more shower clouds.

Such icy and snowy conditions today would probably cause services to be cancelled on safety grounds but thirty years' ago we didn't have such concerns. My adventures that memorable New Year's Day of 1979 would stretch to an article; suffice to say this shot of No.24 running round at Tenterden Town, in the style of Ivo Peters, remains a favourite and one of the finest that I've ever taken. You can feel the cold!

Snegurochka (Snow Maiden) – the misalliance of Spring and Frost – combines with Steam, to produce a rather special scene of 32678 approaching Tenterden Town with a service during Open Day, 27th February 2005.

TWO TO TANGO

Some of the more difficult types of train pictures to attempt involve more than one engine or train. Quite apart from the element of luck – weather, human intervention, presence of steam – the angle taken is often limited and has to be much more precise.

With both engines approaching the end of their current boiler certificates, 376 "Norwegian" arrives at Northiam with the 3.25pm from Bodiam whilst "Wainwright" as WD1960 waits in the Up Platform to return the empty "Wealden Pullman" stock to Tenterden Town. The object here was to get the two engines almost side-by-side, using the white line of the platform edge as a framing guide, and in this case eliminate public inclusion to concentrate attention on the engines. 23rd October 2005. See also page 109.

Viewed from the balcony of the L&NWR Balcony Saloon, 'correctly' marshalled at the Robertsbridge end of the Vintage Train, sees 32678 on the 2.20pm from Tenterden Town whilst No.23 "Holman F Stephens" works through Wittersham Road with the 2.15pm off Bodiam on 31st May 2006. It was taken before No.23 passed the signal in order to emphasise that it was on the moving train.

During the Colonel Stephens' Weekend in 2007, the opportunity arose to obtain a picture of both the Israel Newton reboilered Terriers in action side-by-side. Although the light was less than perfect, this 'event' photograph of W8 "Freshwater" with "Bodiam" piloting 753 on the 4.58pm from Bodiam on 5th May was definitely not one to be missed.

Just over half an hour later, the weather had improved so there was early evening sunshine to greet visiting J15 65462 on loan from the North Norfolk, arriving with the mixed train on the 5.36pm from Bodiam. W8 "Freshwater" was in the loop to remove the freight wagons from the train which then ran as a passenger working back to Tenterden Town.

NORTHIAM UPSIDE

In overcast conditions, the Up Platform, or No.2, can present alternative locations particularly when passing trains in the station.

376 "Norwegian" is observed departing with the Vintage Train for Tenterden Town with the 3.25pm whilst WD1960 "Wainwright" waits with the empty coaching stock of the Sunday Luncheon "Wealden Pullman" to follow it back to Tenterden on 23rd October 2005. In a busy scene, the fence and signals provide an element of framing to the composition and there is unobtrusive human interest on the platform. In an ideal world, WD1960 would not be behind the signal; the idea was to show what can be achieved in less than perfect conditions for subject and weather.

Another view of the J15 0-6-0 on loan from the North Norfolk Railway, this time an away shot of it departing for Tenterden Town with the 3.45 service on 5th May 2007.

The Beattie Well Tank once more, 30587, on 15th March 2008, seen from between the platform and the level crossing with the 3.28pm Bodiam to Tenterden Town.

An unplanned and therefore unadvertised alteration to the Branch Line Weekend at the beginning of July 2006 turned into a mini-Terrier Gala due to the unavailability of P-class 753, which needed repairs. With "Bodiam" required for the Vintage Train, 32678 therefore worked the mixed. In the cooler and overcast conditions on Sunday 9th, with Maunsell coach CK No.56, originally Southern No.5618, providing suitable passenger accommodation, the train made a fine sight leaving for Tenterden Town.

ROUND ORPIN'S CURVE

In spite of the construction of the siding, the 90-degree or so curve on leaving Rolvenden for Tenterden
Town remains a popular area for all photographers.

On Orpin's Occupation Crossing, No.24 "Rolvenden" appears out of the forming mist whilst the evening sun catches the exhaust.
The returning 2.30pm Santa Special of 4th December 2005.

Above: On a lovely autumn day in 2003, DS238 "Wainwright" is seen on Orpin's Occupation Crossing with the 4.30pm from Bodiam to Tenterden Town.

Left: No.24 "Rolvenden" with the empty stock from the Sunday Luncheon running of the "Wealden Pullman", heading back to Tenterden Town, storms round Orpin's Curve on 21st October 2007. The emphasis here is very much on the autumn light catching the exhaust rather than train itself.

The second visit of "Fenchurch" to the K&ESR in preservation occurred in the autumn of 2002. The engine is presented as recently restored to A1 condition, the formal designation for the class by Douglas Earle Marsh prior to rebuild, hence the suffix 'X'. It is painted in Marsh Umber with a pseudo-number; the Duplicate List assignation that it would have carried had it not been sold/transferred to Newhaven in 1898. Still retaining its name on the side of its tanks, "Fenchurch" pilots 753 round Orpin's Curve on the approach to the Occupation Crossing with the 10.40am from Tenterden Town on 5th October, providing the very rare, if not unique, sight of a double-headed train with both engines facing Robertsbridge.

ON TENTERDEN BANK

Although facing an uphill grade round Orpin's Curve, Tenterden Bank starts proper with a short straight section from the vicinity of the Rolvenden Down Home Signal which continues to Tenterden Town for more than a mile at an average gradient around 1-in-50.

DS238 was repainted in early 2005 as WD1960 but retained the "Wainwright" nameplates. On 1st May 2005, the engine is seen hard at work coming off Orpin's Curve at the very foot of Tenterden Bank proper with the 2.15pm Bodiam to Tenterden Town.

"Pastoral Symphony". No.14 "Charwelton" on a goods train is captured in the perfect High Weald setting, having emerged from the Wet Cutting on Easter Monday, 31st March 1997. The Kent (Romney) ewe had only recently given birth to triplets, a rare occurrence for this breed.

32678 and 753 double-head the 1.45pm Santa Special downhill immediately below Cranbrook Road Level Crossing on 4th December 2005.

The empty stock working from Wittersham Road of the Vintage Train seen earlier behind "Bodiam" on 29th December 2007 was also photographed amidst the trees immediately east of Cranbrook Road crossing. Just after mid-day, as the track curves to run a little south of due east, it was possible to get the train in sunshine, with enough light just catching the rim of the smokebox door and handle.

Continuing to curve to the right is a fairly open short stretch of track, seen previously elsewhere in this book, and much favoured by photographers. From the set-aside field adjacent, for a change, a pristine plume of exhaust from No.25 "Northiam" looks brilliant-white against the blue sky of 17th December 2006 with the returning 12.15pm Santa Special.

Same location, but back at trackside is 753 once more in action, this time with a short freight, the 12.58pm Rolvenden to Tenterden Town during the event to mark 50 years since closure to passengers. Whilst a bit of an ugly duckling compared to their Brighton step-cousins, they are a little more sophisticated, certainly benefit from a roomier cab and very much look the part on mixed or short goods trains. 28th March 2004.

753 works the Vintage Train down the Bank with the 2.35pm to Rolvenden during the celebrations to mark the centenary of Tenterden Town Station on 16th March 2003. The train has just passed the Home Signal, with the Parish Church of St Mildred's dominating the surrounding area.

The view from in and around Tenterden Town Station has diminished over the years, the Rogersmead housing estate notwith-standing. So for a final scene in this section it is back to 3rd April 1983 for this barnstorming view of No.14 "Charwelton" pilot-ing No.22 "Maunsell" just past the Home Signal with the 5.15pm from Wittersham Road.

OUT IN THE COUNTRY
In this section is a selection of scenes taken south and westwards from Rolvenden.

Sometimes some of the best pictures are purely reactionary. For the first view obtained on 29th December 2007 of "Bodiam" with the Vintage Train, I remembered a spot near Puddingcake Lane off Rolvenden Hill to the west of the line I'd tried many years before. It paid off handsomely for this quite beautiful rural scene with the sun emphasising the exhaust and countryside to effect.

In its alternative guise of WD191 and suitable camouflage livery, No.23 emits a plume of white smoke in the cold autumn air as it hauls the 2.33pm Hexden Bridge to Tenterden Town between Newmill Bridge and Gazedown Wood on 3rd November 1985.

From the Santa Specials season of 2005, we again see 32678 piloting 753, this time along Oxney Straight on the approach to Wittersham Road, with the 1.45pm from Tenterden Town on 4th December.

Opposite: No.25 "Northiam" propels one of the first trains to Hexden Bridge with the 11.30am from Tenterden Town on 8th May 1983.

A second view of the BTH "Ford" Diesel with the 11.05am from Tenterden Town on 4th November 2006, shortly after crossing Hexden Bridge. Whilst away shots are not to everyone's taste, they can be very expressive of trains in the landscape as this view of the Rother Levels illustrates.

The shortage of motive power and stock on Easter Sunday, 23rd April 2000, meant that 2678 was pressed into service to work a truncated "Wealden Pullman", together with the South Eastern Railway six-wheel brake of 1898. Viewed from the bank of the River Rother, the train wends its way towards Northiam on a slight embankment not far from the former Dixter Halt.

High summer in the Rother Valley. A few times since 2000 I have continued a walk from Bodiam along the banks of the River Rother, which is technically illegal, all the way to Newenden and then back to Northiam Station. Actually, it would make a superb Permissive Path! In the high summer of 2001, the date is unrecorded, one such walk was rewarded by this unusual picture of a pair of swans with their surviving (?) two cygnets serenely paddling along the waterway as DS238 "Wainwright" heads for Northiam with a mixture of passenger stock.

About a mile from Bodiam Station and the classic K&ESR location that was such an inspiration to get the railway rebuilt. "Bodiam" came up trumps again, not for the first or last time on 29th December 2007. This time she is working the 1.00pm from Tenterden Town with the Vintage Train; I had deliberately wanted to make the angle as tight as possible, even if it meant losing part of the train, especially the balcony saloon, which, if populated, would have been a distraction.

The ubiquitous run-past beloved by the photographic fraternity sees "Stepney" with its mixed train on the 'Brighton Works' Sentimental Journey of 8th May 2006, running past the avenue of trees about a third of a mile outside Bodiam. The fact the sun is at a slight adverse is irrelevant; the exhaust is perfectly placed to help create a most charming scene.

On Sundays in January 2001, the railway tried out a low-key shuttle service between Northiam and Bodiam in a style very reminiscent of the Thameside 'Steam at Bodiam' events twenty years previously. No.24 "Rolvenden" is captured in the mid-winter sunshine from the bank of the River Rother with Ewhurst Green in the background on one of these trains; the parish church is dedicated to St James the Great. Poor patronage sadly meant this enterprise was never repeated.

THE VINTAGE TRAIN

Previously marketed as the Victorian Train, a change was forced in 2004 with the entry into service of the Woolwich coach. Whilst not making any claims to originality or uniqueness, whatever formation is on use on any particular day is very much in the tradition of a Light Railway, especially when worked by the P-Class or a Terrier.

No.100 is one of those delightful K&ESR idiosyncrasies. Introduced into service as long ago as 1980, having been discovered in use at Dymchurch, Kent, as a storage shed, it was originally thought to be a District Railway coach. However, several overhauls down the line, the consensus of opinion suggests it was once a longer structure, possibly a Metropolitan coach. It proved to be a catalyst for various subsequent restoration and renovation schemes and whilst often attached to a string of Mark One coaches in the earlier days, now regularly takes its place in the Vintage Train.

Perhaps a bit of an oddity is the vehicle known as the Woolwich coach, built for the London & North Western in 1911 as No.7965. It is a three-compartment brake, which rather restricts its comfortable passenger capacity to less than the nominal 30. Its presence, though, ensures the authenticity of the Vintage Train when GER No.197 is unavailable. It was the first passenger vehicle acquired by the preservation scheme, and was returned to service in 2004 thanks to a benefactor and a Millennium Commission grant. Sold to the Woolwich Arsenal around 1940, its one claim to fame is that Winston Churchill may once have travelled in it.

132

K&ESR No.61 is a SE&CR (South Eastern & Chatham) "Birdcage" brake coach No.1100, so-called because of the prominent raised lookout for the guard, a variation on a theme witnessed on many older coaches in preservation. It came from a set of three sold to the Longmoor Military Railway by the Southern during the Second World War; the other brake also survives on the K&ESR and saw some use after reopening in 1974. At the time of writing, it is nearing the end of a complete rebuild, being finished in early BR red, sponsored by Geoff Silcock's Sentimental Journeys. It will also be used in mixed trains and special workings, principally with the BR-liveried 32678.

A brake vehicle that has proved immensely popular for photographic charters comes from the Great Eastern, very much in the tradition of Colonel Stephens! Indeed its very occasional absences from traffic since entering service in 1991 had forced hybrid use of other vintage carriages with bogie stock until the appearance of the Woolwich and now the Birdcage. Dating from 1887, No.197 originally had two compartments either side of a luggage compartment. Discovered at Wisbech, Cambridgeshire, early restoration was carried out by the Thameside Area Group.

Perhaps my favourite, being fairly contemporary with the P-class, is K&ESR No.88, the former SE&CR No.2947 2nd class four-compartment coach, now designated 3rd class. It was built at Ashford in 1901, the same year as "Bodiam" arrived on the Rother Valley. In service, it was used on suburban trains until rendered obsolete and withdrawn in 1921. We have the late Eric Graves and his Ashford Group colleagues to thank for this superb vehicle, being discovered as one of four forming a bungalow in Kingsnorth, Ashford. It entered service in 1995.

134

Another gem, also built by the L&NWR, is the Inspection Saloon, sold to the Army in May 1940. It saw service on the Longmoor Military Railway from 1945 to closure in 1969 when it was presented to the Transport Trust. Moved to the Severn Valley Railway in 1971, it was transferred to Tenterden with its two companions from the LMR in 1985. An inaugural and integral component of the Vintage Train, it is however less than popular with lineside photographers when marshalled at the Tenterden end of the set. It also provides extra First Class accommodation with bogie stock on the Santa Specials.

Fondly now referred to as the Family Saloon, the second of the 'Longmoor Saloons' and very much the flagship vehicle of the Vintage Train, is the former No.177, built by the SE&CR at Ashford in 1900. Originally it was intended by hire by the wealthy, but as early as 1907 was converted for use as an Invalid Saloon. Also arriving via the LMR and SVR in 1985, it has been a regular in the Vintage Train since 1994 and seen work on the Santa Specials.

THE ROYAL TRAIN

The 9th June 1982 was a very special day for the railway welcomed Her Majesty Queen Elizabeth The Queen Mother to inaugurate "Petros", a converted Mark One coach, modified for the use of disabled persons.

General view from the signal box as No.25 "Northiam", turned to face Robertsbridge, waits with the Royal Train watched by enthusiastic visitors.

No.25 "Northiam" departs Tenterden Town for Rolvenden with the Royal Train conveying Her Majesty Queen Elizabeth The Queen Mother on 9th June 1982.

LE TOUR DE FRANCE

"Bodiam" had managed to miss out on all the major events on the railway, apart from the official reopening on 1st June 1974 but even then it was "Sutton"(Whitechapel) as the south-facing engine that really grabbed the glory. But on Sunday 8th July 2007, the little engine finally had its day in the sun when TV pictures of it posed with the Vintage Train just below Cranbrook Road crossing were beamed around the world thanks to Le Tour de France.

No.3 "Bodiam" takes water a Northiam prior to working a special train to Rolvenden and Tenterden Town for visitors and spectators.

General view of Northiam Station from the level crossing with "Bodiam" about to depart with the Vintage Train.

"Bodiam" leaving Northiam Station on the approach to the level crossing with the Vintage Train on the delayed 09.45am departure to Tenterden Town. Le Tour de France is regarded as marking the first occasion since reopening of the railway providing a genuine transport function.

Ironically, five weeks' later on Sunday 12th August, No.3 and the Vintage Train again had an interesting service to perform, providing a connection from Tenterden Town to Northiam for "Wealden Pullman" customers due to the A28 being closed at Newenden Bridge for scheduled repairs!

WHEN THE SUN GOES DOWN

A feature of traffic on the K&ESR is that with the exception of the "Wealden Pullman" at the height of summer, the only time of year that such photographs are regularly possible, is during the Christmas and New Year period.

I'm not a great fan of silhouettes and neither the pattern of operation nor geography is conducive to such scenes on the K&ESR. However, in 1983, before the siding was built on Orpin's Curve, between the A28 and the Occupation Crossing, the timetable, a clear day and USA No.22 "Maunsell" combined just after the clocks went back to permit me to capture this exquisite picture heading the 4.15pm mixed train on 29th October.

'…For A Moment Like This'. Momentarily brushed with a bronze blush, 32678 pilots 753 on the returning 2.30pm Santa Special, rounding Orpin's Curve on 18th December during that remarkable 2005 season. The exhaust has the impression of being lit from below.

Above: 32678 turns from black to gold in the early evening sunshine as she drifts downhill just below Cranbrook Road Level Crossing once more with 753 on 4th December 2005, this time with the 3.15pm Santa Special from Tenterden Town.

Right: Back on Orpin's Curve as the light starts to fade, it was a question of noticing the reflection off the rails to get the best possible chance of a reasonable picture of "Bodiam" working the Vintage Train on the 2.15pm from Bodiam on 29th December 2007. Though the lack of exhaust cannot be legislated for, the telegraph pole helps add height; the whistle board is for the Occupation Crossing.

Overleaf: Valediction – a fond and final farewell as the returning 2.30pm Santa Special of 4th December 2005 disappears into the evening mist.

…AND FINALLY

To enjoy a meal on the "Wealden Pullman", to watch "Bodiam" pound up Tenterden Bank with the Vintage Train, to see "Norwegian" from a distance working a service train across the Rother Levels, to witness the anticipation on children's faces awaiting a Santa Special, take in the varied sights of a Gala or just to enjoy the railway on a humdrum service, true to its roots, as part of a day out at the castle: these are simple pleasures that in an increasingly unstable, even dangerous world, we should not take for granted.

Taking in the pages of this book, of photographs taken over 30 years and spanning four decades, I am moved to paraphrase and transpose slightly (railway for regiment) the words of General Ames in letter to his former command, the 20th Maine, towards the end of 1863. "…a railway which knows no superior…to which I entertain the most profound sentiments of pride and affection – it causes greater pleasure than I can express."

Fewer than 400 men sweated their way up a small round hill on the second day of Gettysburg as part of a larger enterprise, and marched into history; an insignificant little railway in a corner of the Kentish Weald has survived against seemingly impossible odds on many occasions, and all this in spite of being seen by some commentators over the years as a bit of a joke. Its position as a railroad, in terms of the country as a whole may be small, let alone within the tourist industry on which its future continues to depend, but this does not mean that is contribution to the local economy or the well-being of the human soul should be underestimated.

The sentiment of Ames' original words still hold good, but the K&ES now deserves a different emphasis:
"This is a hell of a <u>railway</u>."